# Games
# Rednecks
# Play

# Games Rednecks Play

## Jeff Foxworthy and Vic Henley

*illustrations by David Boyd*

LONGSTREET PRESS, INC.

Atlanta, Georgia

Published by LONGSTREET PRESS, INC.,
a subsidiary of Cox Newspapers,
a subsidiary of Cox Enterprises, Inc.
2140 Newmarket Parkway
Suite 118
Marietta, Georgia 30067

Printed in the United States of America

3nd printing, 1994

ISBN 1-56352-165-2

This book was printed by Data Reproductions, Rochester Hills, Michigan.

Cover and book design by Jill Dible

*To my brother Jay, for all the games
and laughs we've shared.*

Jeff


*To my big love, my wife Robin—
Thanks for putting up with me.*

Vic

# INTRODUCTION

**W**hen Atlanta, Georgia, was selected as the site for the 1996 Olympic Games — which marks the 100th anniversary of the modern–day Games — a lot of highbrows were raised. Why Atlanta, they questioned, instead of Athens, Greece, where the games supposedly originated?

To anyone who knows a speck of history, locating the centennial Games in the South — a breeding ground for Rednecks — made perfect sense. As long as there have been homemade whiskey and a little free time, Rednecks have been world leaders in creating fun and games. And just like their ancient Greek predecessors, Rednecks have often amused themselves while wearing togas, and sometimes less.

You can look it up in the dictionary if you don't believe it. Mr. Webster defines a game as "any test of skill, courage, or endurance." He also defines the word as "lame or injured," and whenever Rednecks are involved, the two usually go hand in hand. Another definition of *game* is "animals that are hunted." The dictionary does not specify the type of weapon, but whether it's a gun or a truck, Rednecks fill the bill.

The main purpose of a game, however, is amusement, and what could be more amusing than watching friends hurt themselves doing something stupid?  Fancy equipment is not necessary, just the willingness to laugh and to break an occasional law.  If there's a chance of real danger, all the better.  A broken bone or a bad cut is as good as a medal.

A Redneck's love of a good time is usually equalled only by his or her competitive nature.  And why do they love to compete so much?  The answer is in their genes: they never want to pass up a chance to whip somebody's ass.  What's the use of great skill if you can't rub it in the face of your friends and neighbors?  Whether it was dirt surfing down a hill on a piece of cardboard when you were a kid, cow-tipping through your teens, or pledging your love with spray paint as you got older, the desire to amuse and compete is innate to any true Redneck.  Furthermore, if you're playing, that means you're not working, and that can't be all bad.

Ultimately, however, it's the spirit of the games that counts most.  As every true Redneck will attest, it's not whether you win or lose, it's whether or not you'll have a good story to tell later on.

So kick your shoes off, prop your feet up, get yourself something cold to drink, and enjoy this rundown of the *Games Rednecks Play*.

Let the games begin!

# Games
# Rednecks
# Play

# Water Sports

*Platform Diving* —
A good set of rear shocks with a rock behind the wheel and you're in business. The first diver must be a man of honor, as subsequent divers will invariably ask, "How deep is it?" High-top tennis shoes were added as a safety precaution in the late '50s after Dave "Bigfoot" Lipham lost three toes when landing on a rusty beer can at the bottom of Lake Martin.

***Community Pool Diving*** — Favorite dives include: the watermelon, cannonball, belly buster, preacher seat, and — everybody's favorite — the nutcracker. A basic rule of thumb is, "The wetter the judges, the better you score." Record: In 1968, Tiny Wilkes, 485 lbs., did a perfect cannonball and drowned a judge. Scored a perfect 10 but was charged with murder.

***Bridge Jumping*** — What better way to scare oncoming traffic? Scale a bridge, wave at the approaching car, then fall off the side. Make sure you check for stumps below water level, because life in a neck brace is seldom worth an afternoon of stardom.

***3-Meter Springboard*** — Why sink $79.95 into a nice pool if you're just gonna let the kids play in it?

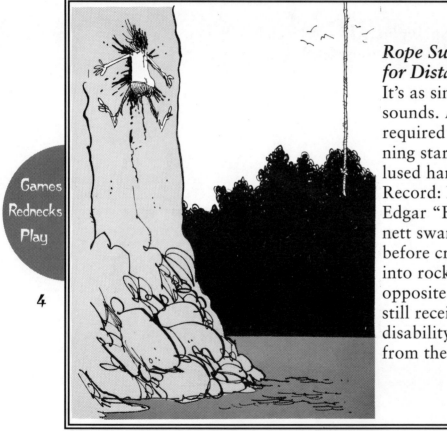

***Rope Swinging for Distance —*** It's as simple as it sounds. All that's required is a running start and callused hands. Record: In 1972, Edgar "Evil" Bennett swang 122 feet before crashing into rocks on the opposite bank. He still receives a nice disability check from the state.

***Rope Swinging, Artistic*** — All-time champion, Corndog Ray, has been described as "Baryshnikov in a pair of cut-off jeans." His two gainer with a half twist, while cutting his toenails, is a signature move that all envy. Corndog's motto is, "The more girls that are watching, the better I am." The Stumbo sisters once inspired him to do the only 3 1/2 with 3 twists, better known as "The Electron," ever performed . . . and survived.

***Trot Line Division*** — The slowest but most rewarding of the fishing events. Crowds are usually small for the actual competition, since most of it occurs at night. But record crowds always turn out for the awards ceremony, where the catch is fried.

**50-Yard Dog Paddle** — Ducks in the water and you've got to get them. Webbed feet and a wide mouth are big pluses in this sport, and champion Ricky Waters has both. Ricky trains Labrador retrievers in the off season.

***Breast Stroke* —** Rarely witnessed but often talked about, most stories open with the words, "This old gal. . . ." The heavyweight divisions are by far the most popular, although Tammy "Pert and Perky" Bonner had developed a huge following in the early '60s.

*Chicken Fights* — The object of this game is to topple your opponents by pushing, shoving, and clawing. In the mixed doubles event, where girls ride on the men's shoulders, you also get the bonus of a possible lost bathing suit top. Plus, there's no better way to take over a Holiday Inn pool.

*8-Man Crew* — The most important thing to remember in this sport is that boat speed equals lure speed. One miscast into a tree is all it takes to eliminate an entire team.  On the other hand, snagging the bumper of a passing 18-wheeler can take you from worst to first in a hurry.

*Sculling* — A precision sport. Just the right touch can produce a few hours of peace and quiet, but too much force can result in a murder rap.

*Rowing* — Not the most popular sport because most Rednecks agree that, "If you can't afford a motor, you can't afford a boat." A good rowing team, however, can pull a skier. It has been proven in competition that urinating off the side of the boat, while always good for a laugh, can cost valuable time.

***Bobbing for Corn —***
Requires strong teeth
and good pores.
Originated in large
families during the
depression.

*Free-Style Skiing* — Rednecks say everything is more fun when you're naked. If it's attention you crave, this sport is the answer. However, performances are less impressive if the water is cold.

***Skipping Rocks*** — The oldest and most traditional of all the Redneck games, although usually not a crowd pleaser. Young turks are trying to breathe new life into the sport by using high tech synthetic ricochet discs (SRD's). The heavyweight division is definitely the most difficult level, as contestants try to skip bricks.

***Cleaning Fish*** — A sharp filet knife and constant awareness of your fingers are essential in this sport. Generally considered an outdoor sport, it is a cheap way to feed the cats, and the scales give the kids something shiny to play with.

# Track and Field

*Flinging* — Originated by an ancient Redneck trying to clean his yard. A great fling is not only a beautiful thing to watch, but often it is accompanied by the exciting sound of something breaking.

DAVID BOYD

***Modern Pentathlon*** — The winner is the one who gets furthest through the entire *Penthouse* magazine library without having to excuse himself. Lewd comments and suggestions are a tactic many use to weaken their opponents: "Troy Boy, she's trying to take your picture!" can send a lesser competitor scurrying for the bathroom. Tim "Nerves of Steel" Jackson is the only champion ever under the age of 55, and his title was revoked after he was found to be legally blind.

*Pole Vault —*
Rednecks decided
years ago to nail
down the crossbar
to keep contest-
ants from knock-
ing it off. This
makes a "miss"
much more
exciting. Any
competitor that
misjudges the
height can walk
and talk funny
for years.

**Hammer Throw —**
A good hammer throw is
almost always immediately
proceeded by a smashed
thumb and a shouted expletive.
However, points may be
deducted for hitting
windows or living
things. Roofers
dominate this game.

***Long Jump —***
This sport is a
Redneck favorite,
since they all own
numerous sets of
jumper cables and
all their vehicles
have dead or
dying batteries.

18

**Bowling Ball Throw** — Big brother to the shot putt. Mabel "Moms" Maloney was the first to demonstrate it after missing a 5-10 split that would have put her over 100 for the first time. Management later adopted the sport as an effective way to break up a crowd at closing time.

**Broom Handle Throwing** — A derivative of the javelin toss. Originated by lazy old men who would throw brooms when dogs wandered into the garden. One of the handles stuck in the ground, and a new sport was born.

***Broad Jump —***
Mercy upon those who fall
short. It ain't pretty.

***High Jump*** — This sport got its start in prison as part of an early self-release program. Records set by prisoners have since been disqualified because gunshots and pursuing dogs have been ruled excessive in their motivational value.

***4 x 4 Relay*** — Remember, always downshift when passing the baton.

***4 x 4 100-Yard Dash*** — All contestants drive monster trucks with tires at least 5 feet tall. Unlike most sprint races, objects on the track only make this more exciting. Who needs steroids when you have nitro?

***Triple Jump*** — Barefoot on hot asphalt in a strip-mall parking lot on a summer afternoon — what other motivation do you need? Record: 92 feet, set by thin-skinned Jackie Sparks in Phoenix, Arizona, on August 6, 1987. He was up and walking again in less than a week.

*Hitchhiking* — Who needs a car when you've got a thumb? For women, cleavage is a great asset. For men, say yes to shirts and no to axes.

*2 x 4 Relay* — Originated at night on construction sites by people looking to expand their homes at low-budget prices.

*Field Hockey* — Who can
run the farthest through a
cow pasture without stepping
in "you know what"? Requires
a supreme sense of balance,
sight, and smell to be a
champion. Shoeless
Walker won 11
straight titles. A
great way to
take the
"new" out of
a pair of
shoes. A really
exciting game
when played at
night with flashlights.

***International Red Rover*** — Dominated for years by people from Wisconsin — milk makes big bones and other things. You always hear the crowd roar when the challengers call, "Red rover, red rover, send Bertha right over!" Bertha once dislocated fourteen shoulders in a single charge.

***Six-Mile Stroll*** — The record is 3 weeks, 4 days, 19 hours, and 23 minutes. The longer you take, the better it is. Style points are awarded based on how many people you stop and talk to, wave at, or admire the babies of. Veterans of this sport have often grown full beards during the competition.

***Mare-a-thon*** — Contestants get drunk and see who can stay on a horse the longest. Great champions always have a butt rash.

***Cow Tipping*** — What could be more fun than terrifying some livestock?  But be sure to wear old clothes and shoes, because the exhaust from a cow hitting the ground can be deadly.

***Tree Climbing*** — All-time champion Dud Colbert — "quick as a cat and almost as smart" — credits his success to strong, thick toenails, a family trait. A sport where excess body fat can land you in the emergency room. As they say, "Don't send a fat boy up a tree if you're gonna stand underneath."

***Hide 'n' Seek*** —
Restricted to
contestants serving
10 years or more.
The player hides
while the sheriff
and his dogs seek.

*Bottle Throwing* — The keys to hitting road signs from a moving vehicle are a strong arm and a steady foot. Veterans will tell you anything bigger than a speed limit sign is for sissies. The record is held by Slingin' Sammy Krenshaw, who hit 34 consecutive mile marker signs with 6 oz. pony beer bottles.

*Standing Long Jump* — Originated when Otis Stratford had to find a way to reach the sofa and the remote control without touching his wife's freshly mopped floor.

# Shooting and Hunting

***Hat Shooting*** — A competition between two Rednecks, usually preceded by some serious drinking. Going first is a BIG advantage, since the second contestant some-times is too dead to take his turn.

MY TURN NOW?

*Synchronized Hunting* — This sport began in an overcrowded dove field — too many hunters and not enough birds.

*Random Shooting* — Rednecks shoot everything, including the bull, the breeze, birds, moons, deer, skeet, rats at the dump, noises, "No Hunting" signs, and each other. The field in this event is usually thinned out during the competition.

*Archery* — Sometimes a firearm is not appropriate . . . especially when hunting on someone else's property without permission.

***Snake Catching —*** There's a fine line between bravery and stupidity, and nothing exemplifies that more than this sport. "Hey, Ed, stick your hand down this hole and let's see if there's something in it!" is this sport's call to arms.

*Alligator Wrestling* — Free shoes, handbags, briefcases, and boots for all the champions. Begun by the Rednecks wanting to prove once and for all that Florida belongs to people and we're prepared to defend it.

*Tracking* — We're not talking about following a blood trail — a sissy sport, according to most pro trackers. A good tracker can trail a grasshopper down the interstate. A favorite put-down in the sport is, "He couldn't track a slug across a sheet of glass."

*Hog Calling* — The good ones can bring a sow into Times Square using only their voice. The *great* ones are often the victims of sexual assault by live pork, which is not a sight for the weak at heart. Record held by Harriet Bellows, who says she merely imitates the sounds her husband Ned makes in the heat of passion.

***Shining Deer*** — "But judge, I work days" won't serve as a defense if you're found guilty of using a high-powered light to spot an animal in his natural habitat (an open field) and put him into an unnatural habitat (your deep freeze).

***Chicken Catching*** — Speed, stamina, and agility are all required for this traditional classic. Whether it's daytime in your own yard or night-time in someone else's, this game also requires a strong stomach for the grisly conclusion.

# Fashion

***Tightest Jeans*** —
Champions frequently
pass out due to loss of
circulation, and some
Hall of Famers have
been confined to
wheelchairs. Always
a crowd pleaser, this
competition can be
very keen.  Judges often
have to resort to the
"scrape test," where
a credit card is scraped on
the contestant to see if it's
denim or body
paint.

YOU KIDS DON'T GET TOO CLOSE NOW... THAT ZIPPER COULD BLOW AT ANY TIME...

FOXY

*Applying Makeup While Driving* — Whether it's the wide-open interstate division or the stop-and-go difficulty of the car pool, each woman must apply a complete layer of makeup (foundation, lipstick, and blue eyeshadow) without removing her cigarette and without smacking the car in front of her.

*Blackest Roots for the Blondest Hair* — Arguably the most popular of all women's sports. Judges have been threatened, slapped, spit on, and even bitten by these self-described "Foxy Ladies."  One of the oldest events, it began when women first realized that men are always attracted to shiny objects.

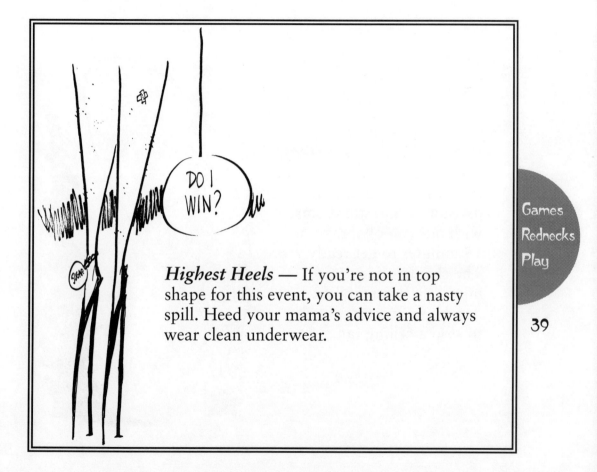

***Highest Heels*** — If you're not in top shape for this event, you can take a nasty spill. Heed your mama's advice and always wear clean underwear.

***Highest Hair or Best Tease*** —
Medals go to the teaser and
the teasee in the doubles
division. Contestants start
with one can of spray and
15 minutes to get ready.
The champion is deter-
mined by flammability,
durability, and most likely
to stop a ceiling fan.

*Shortest Shorts* — There's a fine line between a winner and a flasher. Cut it too close and you could be facing jail time. This is another sport dominated by women, at least in the lower weight divisions.

*Curling* — The divisions range from pink sponge rollers all the way up to coffee cans. Contestants are disqualified if they fail to remain in public less than the minimum of 8 hours.

# Motor Sports

***Creeper Luge*** — Originated after work on Fridays when business was slow at the Hilltop Garage. This sport can be really exciting when there's a busy intersection at the bottom of the hill.

*Tire Changing* — Rednecks and flat tires go together like potatoes and gravy. Rednecks rarely buy more than one new tire at a time, so the threat of a flat is never far away. Alignment is a luxury most can live without. Turnover is high in this sport because most champions end up on NASCAR pit crews.

*Bush-Hogging for Distance* — Put her in drive and hold on tight. A sharp blade and a blatant disregard for personal property are essential to this game. Extra points are awarded for the highest total value of all objects destroyed.

*Mooning* — Whether it's pressed ham against a passenger-side window or a full hang from the rear of a truck, few things match the thrill of making someone else look at your naked rear-end when they're not expecting it. While the moving vehicle category is probably the most popular, the stationary shot still allows the most possibilities. Warning: mooning the elderly, while fun for its shock value, can sometimes send even the strongest pacemaker over the edge.

*Car Rebuilding* — Rules state that cars must remain on your property at all times. Not a sport for the easily bored spectator, as Rednecks often take a lifetime to rebuild a vehicle. Most competitors have multiple cars in various states of repair.

*Shopping Cart Demolition Derby* — When the blue light goes on, the caramel corn starts to fly as Redneck families try to stretch their K Mart shopping dollars.

***Quick Tree Cutting*** —
Style takes a back seat to
speed when getting your
firewood from someone
else's property. A pairs
sport — one loads while
the other one cuts. It's
always a good idea to
leave your own neighbor-
hood to play this game.
For the true thrill seekers,
there's no sweeter sound
than that of a tree falling
on government land.

***Shopping Cart Racing*** — The bag boys' sport of choice. Join them for a death ride as these interlocked, wobble-wheeled locomotives without steering or brakes speed back to the cart corral.

***Tour de Trailer Park*** — Contestants start with brand-new Western Auto bikes loaded with accessories. The winner is he who has the most equipment left after navigating a treacherous course filled with speed bumps and pursuing dogs.

***Cuttin' Donuts*** — Whether it's a neighbor's yard, a vacant lot, or an iced-over mall parking lot, all you need is a carload of friends and a hand-held emergency brake.

***Stealing Signs, Road Cones, or Blinking Lights*** — Pickup trucks and dark clothing are all that's needed as contestants vie to bring home enough stuff to decorate their trailers or apartments. Extras can be kept for graduation gifts.

*Haulin'* — Grab your wife, kids, and dogs, and we're off to the dump. Contestants must also stop and pick up anything of value they may spot along the way.

*Tire Rolling* — You've had a blowout, the spare's got a hole in it, and it's 3 miles to the nearest gas station. "Dear Lord, I'm praying for a downhill exit."

*Hitting Mailboxes with Baseball Bats* — Combine bored teenagers, reliable transportation, and a Louisville Slugger and you've got yourself a game.

# Backyard Events

***Spitting for Distance —***
Strong neck muscles, bad
sinuses, and a good
wind are necessary
to be a champion in this
event. A gap in your
front teeth is also a
big plus. Judges for
this sport are hard to find,
even though they are given a
laundry allowance.

***Clean & Jerk*** — Snatching up a dirty yard rat and holding him or her in a foot-tub until the dirt starts to melt away. Much like washing the dog, often with the same results.

***Peeing for Distance*** — Mainly a male-dominated game, although "Wild Rose" McGee can be a contender if she's had enough to drink. Divisions include parking lot, redwood deck, and hotel balcony.

***Armpit Serenade*** — Players participate in folk, rock, country, and upset stomach noises divisions. Shaving the pits can give off different tones as former champion Dan "Scratchy" Paulding found out on his way to victory in 1976.

*Fencing —*
If there's one
thing Rednecks
know about, it's
fences. We're
not talking that
fancy store-
bought chain
link stuff. Any
man worth his
salt can make a
fence out of
common items
found in his
yard, such as
used appliances,
old pallets, sheet
metal, car doors,
or bailing wire.

***Pig on a Flame —***
After watching the Olympic
Games, Rednecks decided a big
flame that lasted for 14 days could
be put to better use. Besides, nothing
can ease the strain from intense competition better than good bar-b-que.

53

***Homemade Tattoos —*** The sport which begat the phrase, "An idle mind is the devil's work-shop."

***Best Tattoo Design*** — Tough to judge, but many think Slim Hastings' "Elvis and a hula girl on a Harley, on a battleship named MAMA" is a record that may never be broken. The sport's first perfect 10.

***Speed Tattooing*** — Became a much more exciting sport when, due to a rule change, judges began deducting points for incorrect spelling.

***Tattoo Recognition*** — With a tube top covering at least half of the artwork, the contestant must guess the entire tattoo.

***Porch Decoration (Artistic)*** — Contestants start with the same appliances; whoever produces the prettiest grouping is the winner. An arrangement with a viewing of Elvis or Jesus scores big with the judges.

***Porch Decoration (Bulk)*** — Who can get the most junk on their porch in the shortest amount of time. A brother-in-law usually makes a good partner: "Don't throw it away, there's still room on the porch." Bonus points awarded for working appliances.

*Firecrackers* — As champion "Stumpy" Lynch says, "With experience comes missing body parts. But you gotta pay the price to be the champ!"

*"Mercy!"* — Restricted to females 45 and older, this is not a game for the meek. Even the most experienced judges can become unnerved after watching contestant after contestant dab away tears, wring hands, and moan, "Mercy!" The event originated with two middle-aged women telling each other about their "female problems."

*Cigarette Flip* — Filters or non-filters, whoever can flip the farthest with the most revolutions wins. This one's best when played outdoors.

# Miscellaneous

*Weightlifting —*
What better way
to prove one's self
worth than by pick-
ing up something
heavy? Hemorrhoids
and hernias are a
champion's constant
companions.

*Parallel Bars* — Contestants leave the hotel at the same time and try to make it the entire length of Bourbon Street. The first one to Pat O'Brien's, without throwing up, wins.

*Hand Slapping* — Hand-to-hand combat in its purest form. A full crush can draw blood and tears.

*Sabers* — Nothing but a fancy term for a knife fight. A spontaneous sport that usually starts with the challenge, "What the hell you looking at?"

***Vault*** — What's the use of having money if you had to work to get it?  Good competitors drive Cadillacs, while bad ones do hard time.

*Mumblety-Peg or
Knife Throwing —*
It doesn't hurt to
miss every once
in a while just to
shake up your
opponent. That is,
it doesn't hurt your
chances of win-
ning; it may hurt
your opponent a
good deal.

***Body Bowling*** — A hard head and slick silk shirt are big pluses in this event. Coming back through the ball return can be bothersome, but that cool air from the fan is extremely soothing to a bruised and swollen forehead. Champions usually score very poorly on the S.A.T.

***Rasslin'*** — Not that boring Olympic-style wrestling, but real rasslin' like on TV. We're talking no TV time limit, lights out, no holds barred, Texas death match in a steel cage where the loser must leave town with a shaved head.

***Beer Cap Snap*** — Contestants show hand/eye coordination and manual dexterity as they fire at an array of targets, such as roaches or empty cans or bottles on the TV. Two words of caution: too hard a snap can break a picture tube, and bottle caps should be collected at the end of the day, as stepping on them on the way to the kitchen for that middle-of-the-night beer can teach children words that would make a trucker blush.

***Find Your House*** —
Not as easy as it
sounds. After a long
night of drinking
and shooting pool,
most trailers start
to look alike. Bonus
points awarded for
details remembered
the next day.

*Foil* — The first person to get reception on an $89 K Mart TV with only one roll of Reynolds Wrap wins. Reception is a judgment call.

*Quarters* — Extremely difficult to officiate because Rednecks will cheat at a game where only the losers drink.

*Sneakin' In* — Better known as "the mother of all obstacle courses." Contestants must run the gauntlet, beginning with faulty car mufflers and moving through barking dogs, squeaky door hinges, kids' toys in the hall, and — everybody's back breaker — the ironing board in the living room.

***Ear Thumping*** — Best played in the winter. A good thump can render some victims "lobe-less." Hall of Famer "Head" Williams, who completely lost both ears while moving through the amateur ranks, attributes his success to a long, boney, double-jointed bird finger.

***Flinch*** — The ultimate test of nerves as opponents' punches stop inches short of vulnerable body regions.

***Most Children by the Age of 18*** — Adoptions don't count. The more fertile the child, the prouder the grandparents. A grandma by 30? Why not! Escape the boredom of junior high for the excitement of the delivery room.

*Softball* — Nobody cares who wins. The big questions are, "Did you get dirty?" and "Did you get drunk?" If you answer "yes" twice, you had a good time. Most people play just to get a uniform. What better way to show off a beer belly than stretching a polyester shirt that says "Royal Flush Plumbing" across it?

*Written Pledges of Love* — We aren't talking love letters or poems here, but something the whole county can see. There are two divisions: (1) Artistic Expression, which requires more than one can of Krylon, and (2) Repetition, that is, who can cover the most locations per square mile?

*UFO Spotting* — An open mind and a glazed facial expression are the only prerequisites. UFOs are strange critters; you rarely see them if you aren't drinking.

# Discontinued Sports

*Water Polo* — Rednecks tried this only once because too many horses drowned. Besides, any true Redneck caught wearing one of those goofy shower caps would automatically have his fishing license revoked.

*Cricket* — Too many people were squashing them or stealing them for bait.

*Croquet* — Why would anyone waste good bailing wire by just sticking it into the ground?

*Equestrian Events* — These were discontinued in favor of some games played with horses.

*Post-Hole Digging* — Discontinued because contestants would borrow them and never bring them back.